Lent Always Takes Us

Lent Always Takes Us

by David Craig

RESOURCE *Publications* · Eugene, Oregon

LENT ALWAYS TAKES US

Resource Publications
An Imprint of Wipf and Stock Publishers
199 W. 8th Ave., Suite 3
Eugene, OR 97401

www.wipfandstock.com

PAPERBACK ISBN: 978-1-5326-8751-8
HARDCOVER ISBN: 978-1-5326-9643-5
EBOOK ISBN: 978-1-5326-9644-2

Manufactured in the U.S.A.   AUGUST 14, 2019

Contents

Every Knee Shall Bow

Poems begun during Lent

Notes | **59**

Every Knee Shall Bow

Where we live

The back light offers its shadows in night grass,
the wooden fence across the alley. Daylight
is different. Blue skies own us, unmoor us home.

This is beauty we can't know, life beyond our telling.
Jesus, who can speak azure? The color of sun?
What river floats beneath these trees, what fictions?

If I could take you, Friend, with me, I would:
our ambitious tails, the way they slap the sea.
Who could go wrong in such a jocund company?

Did John of the Cross live like this, I wonder?
In this beautiful sunny wasteland, in a palpable wait?
Did he invent what we know of the truest Spain?

Huckleberry is a Finn if you believe it or not.
He expands because he must, because this place
always offers what it can never seem to give.

Give me the row boat's bottom as I shoot, pause.
The problems are still here: you feel the cords of water;
but we can pull, too—can have commerce with early birds.

Bears huddle close in the night cave

They breathe in winter, their noses wet from play.
They trundle in their dreams, going wherever they please.
How could heaven or Christmas be better than this?

Here it's all iodine and the medicine cabinet.
All I hear are voices, the next place I have to go.
There's dirt on my shoes, and the floor's just been mopped.

I want my bear mind. I want winter green,
the sound of icicles swaying, breaking in the trees.
I don't want snowshoes, Black Diamond expedition poles.

The only things we have to recommend us have finished.
They've gone on ahead, leaving a few prints behind;
the stars, making a hymn of winter's white air.

Come stand with me out on Wright's cold corner, Friend.
A Ford putters past, addresses we will never know.
I want my poverty to grow where nothing can feed it.

I want my grown sons to gather, to pull on these ropes.
I want my daughter to taste some pu-erh tea.
Let the streaks of tundra bless the night—what waits.

Our friendship with ruins

Children dance above white moonlit flowers:
pioneers. They can't pronounce the names that own them,
a wrap too skilled, too dense, for them to untwine.

Their mittened hands do not have words enough,
though they speak some owl and barn, some dusty hay.
This is what they've always wanted! The thing beyond them!

It's the place of hope, after all, someone else's craft.
The cocoon always spins us, until the day it cracks.
Then our wings will surprise with their drying texture, spread.

I'll probably want to go dark, back again,
at least once in a while, to lie deep in blackest soil.
I'll want to hear the lip of the first green syllable.

Maybe there'll be a slew of pod people there,
no one giving a thought yet to the sun. Just rain,
softly, as it pock, pocks the dirt around us.

We'll stay right there for a thousand heavenly years,
until we can feel with the worms, croak in the sun:
be both pitcher and bowl, any crack in the sky.

Invitation to soybeans

My wife says it's in everything, hydrogenated oil.
Like estrogen in the water, which will kill my male.
It's enough to make you think that businesses don't care.

We dance our small rooms when the Spirit moves.
No stars come out, the smell of damp wool for company.
(Personally, I'd always hoped for something more.)

Mops, broom handles, a Stooge's comic parade.
Keaton, perhaps, as something skips the gramophone.
(At end, I'll have spent my life in a large closet!)

Sing little bird, outside of the rain this morning.
I've seen you on some days, praising God and man,
the only feet on your bobbing baton—branch.

Perhaps this is how it is, for all of us:
the lone voice, footwork, our morning trills.
A certain earnestness: may it number our remaining days.

The birds, with a kind of instinct, get up, do it
again. So will we. We weigh our world, up and down,
channeling Isaiah, *Mad* Newman, drawing stick figures.

Light winter mist on the Ohio

—driving my daughter back to college

Like an old log, bobbing in a wake, we rise
in the sounds we make. Heaven is all around.
This is how we know that we are still here.

That and the dear voices that fill our days:
people you can touch and yet somehow never can.
We will never fully know our children until heaven.

Still, I'm grateful for any time I get,
anywhere: near the water, in the car—or out.
Now is the only place built for fruitful failure.

What is this sidewalk I walk on, the canvas of my shoe?
This is why I forget so many things, my Friend!
The King has spread his fare for all to see.

I'm waiting for my completion, my modest crown—
while I type this in a cold barefoot motel in Huntington.
I cry "The King is risen," while my family sleeps!

So often, the Truth seems like our small secret.
And so it's always been: one little fool
or another, giving speech to a misty shore.

Playing flute in an empty cistern

is like watching the backs of your hands. It's all you've got.
The notes fade, sweet though they are each time you rise
to do it again. It becomes an anthem, a dirge.

You could do push-ups, recite what you know of the Torah.
It's odd, how the moments you don't act define your life.
(Our rescue always comes from the rope of a fallen brother.)

Any future looks good. You try to be grateful for the minutes,
for the dreams, which keep coming—in an alien caravan.
(It's the little messages that carry us through our days.)

Rest finally comes with a household. You're a slave to the quiet.
Neither the rising nor your fall came from you.
It's the King's jewelry you wear on the best of days,

on the worst. The vacuous noise of it beating against
your chest. Only humility can save you here.
This is how it is for all of us free people.

Joseph was careful, you can bet, for the rest of his days.
He knew better than most how much each penny weighed.
His life was a deprivation, a holy defeat.

The bald eagle and the chemical plants

share the trees, Route 2, in West Virginia.
What do the poor have but what's been given them—
what's been taken away? Still they have the sun,

its iced leavings in January; their old beat-up cars.
(The chrome boardrooms use a faster time.)
We've lived here much longer, know the real names of the rivers.

Our children may get autism or cancers from your food,
but they'll know the music hidden in these old hills.
Mercy sustains them, offers a road they know.

Their songs will include the cross. They'll know money's woe.
They'll live in what they've been given, like all the poor
before them. (She gives her own a sturdy wing.)

This is the West Virginia I have seen:
where the people are made of river shale and angst.
They put up Christmas lights throughout the year.

Come to a church, a Mass; no one will stick out!
Their cry is heaven's own, the voice of coal mines.
They've seen death before you came—will see it go.

Complicity

It is always the same bird. Its name is Robert.
He has no home. He has never had a home.
His song will make you weep: the only song there is.

This land is dead. He cannot make it rise.
Perhaps that is why he sings. You'd have to ask him.
(When Jesus was asked to leave the forum, He left.)

And now dead babies litter the street, on lamp posts.
We sit around and wait for the rest of the dead.
There are no echoes here, little light.

The poets speak among themselves, from beer—
their wrists tied loosely in a passive complicity.
(We all are being escorted, against our wills.)

Flowers lose petals. Compunction no one feels.
We are the line of prisoners we've chosen to be.
Everyone speaks French, but that will not save us.

We can't offer His name here. It's too late for that.
We go to the hell that awaits us. An answer to our crimes,
where mercy is a lie, a factory of fawning dreams.

When Saturn ate reason

Don't blame him for that. It was a long time coming.
Think of those little black shoes, those wigs, standing up
all night on holders, thinking and talking it over.

They gave themselves foul names, extended vacations.
But powder can no longer hurt us. Swift is dead.
We know his reach, the God who came to save him,

Who lives best with spiders, in the sway of dewy nets.
He lives in every barn, in tractors, all farm
machinery: the rust, the pollen, the sprinkler systems.

You have to come to Him. He wears an old hat.
His name is Eugene. He'll hop off to give you a hand,
a Bible. He'll listen as long as you've got something to say.

The tractor noise can go on until late at night.
Then He'll sit back, a bench against the barn.
He'll share His tobacco, talk about what's taking you.

Wind-blown chaff takes the measure of our evenings.
You see the birds, fluid, shaping the high air;
four stiff gloves stacked, like the days and the work to come.

A blue tarp sails through a blue sky

It's the kind of alleluia angels sing
when the cab is late, when the Cubbies have split a pair.
Kids wave flags. Zoos have the necessary mementoes.

Nothing is the way it should be, least of all you.
Your ears are too big. You drink white milk with a straw.
They wouldn't let your kids into the middle school.

It's just as well. The desks are all in a line;
people have to wait their turn. The bathroom has stalls.
I've heard they chain you lockstep—to teach you song.

Leaves flutter outside the occasionally opened windows.
No one can keep them still. They're the children of children;
they fall then rise, create a holy ground.

It always seems better, doesn't it, out there among
the truer vestiges. But there's truth in bad choices too.
Even the slowest pilgrim finds his way home.

He'll bang on some future door, badly dressed;
no one with any sense would let him in.
He'll be loved—sparkling conversation at every turn.

The winter stars are teacups

New snow is a letter sent by a distant friend.
It's a world you cannot contain, a soft envelope
that tells you again that you do not own this house.

We are all boarders, my wife, my children; the home
we create is beams and talk. It's blue powder,
winter again: crystals we kick up to God.

Daylight sparkles in the frigid morning sun.
Your boots discover the white again, the sound,
the crunch that Mass makes in this world of ours.

How many miracles can any of us endure?
I think of a colleague, his beautiful Protestant virtue!
(And my father, giving me a Catholic sip of beer!)

It's the otherness in life that gets us every time:
a glass on a table, my wife coming down the stairs,
the day that waits like Sisyphus in front of us.

A day made just for us, like light snow this morning,
Jesus, rising in the sparkling sun of these hills,
wisps of yes, each more cold than we'd like.

"Someone to Watch Over Me"

Low sun in winter speaks to the green of the lawn.
It graces our cars with a kind of warmth, once removed;
like a walk with memory, it's the good that keeps us in place.

No one else could have made this journey: my spouse, as she plays
"I only have Eyes for You" on the piano, the dog,
baying out—as poems begin their surface.

There's something to be said for age, the deepening of desire.
It finds its place among the shoes, the rack,
the dust in the bay window, its lace curtains.

Jesus, we've become a movie set, a place
where an aging Hollywood deva might come to her senses.
The 30s could live here. (The part that didn't exist.)

Our guest will arrive soon. We'll serve him wine and spaghetti.
Hopefully the old days will snap back, the beers
and father talk. I'll hear about his homeland again.

We rewrite our lives every single chance we get.
You just can't stop us. It's like we're little gods,
trying to make the right world right again.

Getting the band back together

A timbre rolls through a row of the wintery trees,
tambourines under the bright moon. Their tamp
echoes as we woodlings kick up the light fluff.

My daughter would be here, if she were; my past, its line
of regret! It's a sorry tune, as we foot it through
the night, through praises and the names we give ourselves.

Grade school friends salute me! I'd gotten it wrong.
This is a mercy train. We can call ourselves "made new":
a rock-a-billy band, we transform the waiting ferns.

We could be that—or a swarm of pet shop ferrets,
singing our joy: gloving each other. The play,
the sleep. They chant so the trees can sough, drop snow.

Tall angels, they lift each loaded bough in song—
like Wordsworth, walking again through drifty England.
The call always goes out in a nightly silence, doesn't it?

You can hear it make its case in the wrinkling stream,
the park bench. "Yes," each says, speaking earth.
"We've been touched again by the people of God."

The souls in purgatory

Oh brothers in the drudge, how bright and happy must be
your task. It's as if your death had never happened:
you pull with the others, probably share a joke.

"Meet at Phil's," after work. A bock restores the soul.
(By this time you're pushing with your back, your last legs,
running out of gas. But a sister picks you up.)

They must have breaks, the time to listen to bird song,
the sun always just rising, unless you need
a different scene, people quietly passing.

They were, of course, the ones you didn't help.
But they don't mind. Everyone has his oar.
(Someone's doing Dinah Washington far off.)

All have sinned here, each making his long goodbye.
The many detours make the road seem right.
We commit each slip to memory, widen our praise.

The gates will open for everyone, but he won't go there.
Time is not his to waste. It's his tender, Friend.
The past must go, only as it was spent.

Weasel poem

Weasels take to humility. They slide right into it.
Get him wet and no hole is safe, no chicken home.
(The Japanese don't even like him: his cry, bad luck.)

Even when he hides, he can't. He's seen the stares,
the chicken just before he jaws its throat.
His hands are muddy, swift about their business.

He has an altar in his hole, the smallest of crosses,
holy cards; though he prays, alas, alone.
It's he and the night, the stars and his runny nose.

Given his past, where would you expect him to go?
His world is high weeds, sounds of the always other.
He is here for this, a syndicate of repeated crimes.

His sins define him. He wishes it were not so.
So he walks under beautiful stars, in the smallest of houses.
He will never get invited to the country club.

He dips, late, into the stream. His coat shines again.
He tacks up no address by the door of his hole,
finds his ease in a pile of wettest leaves.

The long winter road

—*Thérèse*, the movie

The winter snap, wispy snakes, say you're home.
St. Thérèse lived here. She suffered—wants me to follow.
She reached out to death with both of her young French hands.

God's will was what she knew, in the watch: the next thing
that came. Assent has a fragrance all its own.
Her hands were like open flowers, the end of each day.

She saw our years, walked those palatial tiles,
which is Calvary, our generous gate. She invites us in.
(And who's ever here for himself? For what he can get?)

That's why she carried that cross: to see things through.
Let her joy infect me. Let the angels of deprivation
clothe me in the motley of an anonymous Paradise.

What I've wanted has delayed what still might come:
the quiet that angels make, their comings and goings
as she sewed beads in recreation—a wind.

Jesus has always had the smallest of armies.
They march without fear because they know Whom they serve.
You can hear her, barefooted, still walking around that bed.

St. Valentine's Day

Candied hearts will crack your teeth: "I wuv you."
This is where we live (right off of Route 22).
So I'm holding a bunch of roses—for a smiling cashier.

It's good to go through something (small) for the one
we love, for the one who shows us how to carry the cross.
I should've bought confetti, an elevated chair.

The days go by, and who is there, bringing bags
out of the cold, helicoptering our daughter,
touching base, I hear, with our married Aspi son?

Who knows how we get through the mazes of this world?
Carefully, yes, but mostly through the spousal help
of the dear one tied to the chair of our every woe.

I should give her something every day: a button,
half my dessert. (Some days she takes me up
on *that* proposition, and I must learn love again!)

Every man knows this, whatever her amped up schedule.
Beneath all that movement lurks a saint, still younger
than she. It's something we might live to see.

Burnt Sienna unmade me

Still the bones insist, come back together,
need to be pulled apart again, and again.
This is the function of poetry: to teach us to die.

I am not whole, nor ever will be, here.
The only beauty is my perpetual undoing.
Come shake my zombie hand. Take it with you.

I will become a part of everything I see.
Even on one foot, I'll be able to dance on the grass.
I'll celebrate at weddings, break the Jewish glass.

Our sin slowly makes us whole. We rejoice at the telling
because we're here in snow-white air, a clan
of disappearing ruffians, empty gestures.

The sun, the planets too. Help me unname them.
The first will be "un," the second, already gone!
We will count until our mouths can do no more.

It's like Dickinson, bodied, waiting for a final judgment.
"Have you died yet?" "Me neither." "Let's make a poem!"
Resigned groans will seep from the adjoining tombs.

When I wake up

I want to truly be there, Friend, to be
the one I've been waiting for. A big smile on my face,
I want Babe Ruth's bat and a bottle of Milwaukee.

All my papers will be graded and summer will be coming on.
It'll be beer in the back yard, the best part of the neighborhood
croqueting to the sound of some old time rock 'n roll.

It might not be heaven, but a resting spot for souls
like us. Grandkids will make it over. The smiles
of old ones marking the height of the smallest children.

Either that or we'll get a visit—that sun standing still
for Old Testament patriarchs, who'll teach us games,
regale us with folk song and strange foods.

Then, alas, our cousins will show, tires scraping
the curb. It won't be Jesus coming through the door,
but it won't be all the less we deserve either.

So praise, praise, I say. If He ain't gone,
He's here—thinking just for now that maybe
the apple hasn't fallen that far from the tree.

Loud joy

What was it like on the shores of Galilee?
Would my chickens, scattered, have all come home to roost?
But then, again, I would have seen His Face!

I couldn't do my clown, or run away.
I'd have to walk behind—though He would see,
call me up to the head of the class, for some brother love.

Fear would have no place there. The world needed to see
its origin. God's Ekstasis! Bread everywhere:
in His speech, in the talk of the dead; His freedom in the trees.

People parted like a tide, then gathered behind;
heaven had come, and no one there was the same.
Everything you thought you knew was wrong, too small.

And while it's true that that is there and this
is here, His voice has carried these many years
(such are my yips and yaps, my almost full).

If people only knew the reason why we dance, the reason
why our joy is much larger than we could ever be,
they'd walk without windows, side with the nearest sea.

The sun and all his sundry fellows

It's a golden dance of bears, the rippling gait
as they gallop away. It's early morning in Wyoming,
beer glasses still on the table. Talk is a memory.

One man passed out, half outside the doorway.
It's a cool breeze that serves you up the past.
A good night is never wasted. It will come again.

Your sins are wide as the Mississippi River,
as the birds which accompany you, the saw grass there.
Did you think that you wouldn't get off that easily again?

And can you possibly repay when you live the gift?
Can you give life to the sky, create a woodchuck?
Can you serve the mist that creeps up from the river?

Most of us limp, gross sinners to paradise.
A model for no one, we straggle across the fields.
Rags in the morning, like Shelley's skylarks shooting up.

We have only this moment, Jesus. We give it to You.
Keep us as You have, in the better steps we take—
our slowness of foot is finally Your concern.

Into May

The sun brings new noises to the neighborhood.
It tells you that summer will exact different things:
a certain willingness to expand, to finish each game.

Eventide will demand a dance, a thankful squire
around our smallish physical plant. My Down's son
Jude will want to take the measure of his life.

And who could blame the lad, the birds of heaven,
righting themselves—enough to ignore the air
on Sunday mornings, when the steel mills cough their waste?

We sing because something in us won't give up,
because that is what it means to be alive.
We will not be put off so easily, Friend.

What is bigger, anyway, the bad news or what follows?
No, we will go about our ways in the way
of what's already come. We'll patch our basement,

we'll cut the grass, gather the plates after dinner.
Perhaps I'll smoke a pipe—or walk the dog.
We'll let the day itself decide what's next.

Each drop of groundwater has a home

It doesn't know its name, might take shame some days
from that fact. But on others, its joyfully tests the echoes
in every space. It haunts the world with its life.

The stars are heavenly rumors, the kind he likes best.
They expand him like the rain that trains him in the school
of the real. His verse has a part in the larger song.

It's all part of the passing flood. He must be brave,
be clear about the things he can count on: nothing.
"Oh Great Orion, let your light shine down on me.

I wake and find the dirt I've always known.
I dance when I can in the same restricted place.
Hear my small feet, my bonnet, my buttonhole of joy."

But even if he can't find room, he'll continue to sing.
His name is just spelled that way: one of the many.
Without him, there is no ocean of harmonic praise.

There would be no farm, no animals, no cud, and no voice.
He grows because he can do that, his tiny roll
marks a path others have taken—improves the soil.

Where Jesus lives

Everything here gets worked out, with or without us:
the sun comes up, cats pad a neighbor's lawn.
Our own lives, too, don't belong to us.

This is how Love works. He crowds us out of our lives,
brings our baggage along—just to keep us honest.
We lift a sorry hand to help our neighbors.

We pirouette together, one sinner and the next.
The last dance before the end of the world.
Put a finger on my spinning head. We'll make it new.

We could try a shout, let the rest of the people know,
but who's ever listened to us? Who needs us to change?
Consider this so, Larger Poetry World!

It's not exactly the last Word, but we do know Him:
great beer drinker, calmer of fishboat storms.
His love will make you know the glory of your place.

Come to the fish fry, you can try the washtub bass.
You can untune the sky, talk smack with Dryden.
Or you can make new friends—*then* find cover.

These writer friends who've gathered

around beers and bright talk are acorn barnacles—
or the heat in the furnace of God. We throw in our logs,
almost carefully. Man the hot post, our lies.

Your sins get revealed to everyone around the room,
and not for the first blessed time. God knows this well.
It's a laugh the two of you share around the forge.

They are a rough crowd, these good men with children:
boys gone wrong enough to put us here,
each filled with a hundred stories to pass the time.

What a joy it is to sing to the winter moon,
to go to a dark home, to a sleeping wife,
as charitable as God Himself, the following day.

Jesus is the One who puts us here. May He check
our clumsiness, keep our rousting tongues at play.
May the beer flow again, amid the straggling children.

May we have a part in inventing this enlivening world.
He creaks every late wall, the steps to your bed—
just as He pushed the tires down against the snow.

Small enough to count

St. Francis collected rough stones, each a false self
to be stacked. He had no words for this, never would.
It was the only way the sky could clear:

echoes, rock scraping over stone. The angels
reclined in this blessed grunting—the ease in the trees.
Speech could come after, if it came at all.

The wind said enough. He would be the dirt and the earth.
He would be his angst, a cry he could not control.
(When he got tired—the flowers didn't seem to care!)

The world goes on. So would he by the look of things.
His death was all he could cling to: humility, strife.
How else could he be small enough? He would only subtract.

"Jesus, You know how I am. I'm the one who must die.
My grief will be my blanket; my life, the cold."
Humility was the only stair. It would take him home.

You might say that it could do the same for us,
though someone is going to have to lead that way!
A quiet intransigent, around his generous fire.

Poems begun during Lent

St. Francis, the inmate, slept here

in one of these small swales, a shaded tribute
to the five and dimes of the imagined fifties.
(I could have had the idyllic childhood I wanted.)

But what lasts—cannot, unless it's given leave.
The good these days meanders like a shallow river,
days you throw open, like your Down's son's window.

The two of you could sparkle, driving the Platte.
This morning might be Nebraska, a better spring.
It might be the horses we talk to, a limb on the road.

Chances are, not. I've got to bring me along,
the ashes, my childhood like a string on stripped cans
tied behind me. They make stealth, passage, impossible.

Just as well. The angels know this, us; and they
don't mind. Their world is large and filled with wonder.
Nothing can change that. Each of us, a kind of flower!

St. Francis lived Lent every day of his ragged life.
It was the succor the world could never quite give—
the ease in the trees: a model for what a man might be.

Lent always takes us

however we begin! The work is too deep to be
our own. We'll travel the road as if we know
where we are heading. But we haven't the slightest idea.

That is tomorrow's problem. Today it's prayers
for the dead: a rosary for Steve whose funeral card
I just found, thirty years old in a yellowed book.

I'd mistakenly avoided him at the hospital—the distance,
almost enough to serve as an excuse. Part of me
didn't want to be their praying Catholic seal.

He was our softball right fielder. Whatever his sins,
he was a welcome presence. I feel him in prayer,
want to do whatever I can. May Jesus take him home.

Then I saw his face in my wedding DVD I'd just
come across, dark in the shadows; but it was his profile.
(I speak for the dead whenever I open my yap.)

So here we are, Steve, me and you, the gang,
at Madden's bar. No one lifts 'em high anymore—
except in heaven. I wonder what they drink.

Twigs at the altar, an ashy pate

The grainy thumb delights: it gives you what you came for,
the push of the season, the want buried in flesh.
Death, the mother of virtue, must find her home.

But we know, too, that Thérèse was pushed to her limit.
We are made of less, soldiers gathered late.
Our hands sweat, we stand too lax at the gate.

Still, today is what we have, a voice
to cry God's need. We are thick twigs in the grass:
a knuckled, thin collection of broken promises.

We're birds with too many feathers, creatures He's made!
(We look—could play—no part, could never fly.)
We circle for effect, flapping our talk, our losses.

Fen and fowl, Shakespeare and song, no fairies
protect us here. Oberon is only the moon;
Puck voices the final magic, offers the bard.

We stumble and praise, proceed, ruddy mechanicals,
ass-faced, off-key, under Wednesday's last lights:
God's brilliant design—well past what we could do.

The smaller saints get

the more room they find—they house inside themselves.
They walk the lonely mansions of God, bright marble,
where no one shouts their name, where birds sing mornings

into being. Noons come, and at our back, time's winged
chariot rackets its way down the basement stairs,
reminding us of where our days are spent.

St Joseph works his plane. You make him smile.
That's the only noise that passes between you two.
It's hard to be that quiet; you wait for his speech.

The silent cross rises. You can feel its heft
as it's lifted up all over the neighborhood. It's like
the insides of your life, where you're no good to anyone.

This is where we always start, in a death silence,
where even place has been taken from you. The task—
not given. You might feel the damp ground, but you don't.

St. Joseph will help: breviary, shavings on the porch.
His dreams still lead him. Ours sometimes do the same—
in surreal dream fields, where nothing makes any sense.

Next year in Jerusalem

The terrain is better where you do not matter,
each gouge in the earth is a letter from a distant friend;
night trees seem to withdraw in the cool desert air.

If you want consolation, you just might have to wait
as you walk toward an alien culture you cannot fix—
your footing is slow, because the night is not yours.

There are no comfortable noises among churring insects.
This is where they tied Him, for a different kind of carnival.
You are part of the outsiders. You are also part of the in.

This will never change. It's why you are here again.
You have never been among the greats of the earth.
The kingdom you insist upon does not exist.

So you mill among a people you do not know,
in a place with strange customs, camels and wraps.
It's been like this since you had the face of a child.

Life insists you wait. Not for the things you want,
but so you can see your place in the scheme of things;
you feel the cross as it slides, locks into place.

Homer's Cimmerians

Mist and gloom get bad names. Sunshine is over-rated.
Hope has become a meteorological phenomenon. . . .
We see best in a dimmer light, have dispensed with doors.

The next thing you know, it's the pan flute, the fog
police. They knock on the doorframe, say they're just checking,
but we've all been down this community road before.

What passes, always does: clouds, weathers.
Give me my soul, whatever its bent shape.
How can I know Jesus unless I live in my house?

I have an old hammer, so I can fix my shutters.
The natural light is sometimes enough. Plants grow,
a discarded Chevy almost sparkles in the morning dew.

The dim sun sticks its foot in the door. Well, just so
it doesn't think it owns the jukebox. We can glint
and bear it, until a trace of normalcy returns.

We sharpen sticks in the yard, try to mend our ways.
You can never tell what epic will appear out of fog.
Or else it's the milkman—who always rattles first.

Lent ain't been no purple chair

And so we wait for him again. The unwelcome,
expected guest. He's like the rest of your life.
You wife's given him room to stretch out on the couch.

He's nice about it, lifts his feet so you
can vacuum. He clears off the table after dinner.
Sometimes he sings alone in a back yard night.

You begin to see his life hasn't been easy either,
down to his sin since he got his second sight.
No wonder she kindly took the wayfarer in.

She had no idea as to the length of his stay.
He does not joke. Barely speaks when directly addressed.
He is suffering itself. A comment larger than he.

You can dismiss him, though that would be a mistake.
Other versions take walks all over the happy neighborhood,
each in a hoodie, taking out the recyclables.

You were hoping routine might make him a man of principle.
But that's putting a wheel-less cart before the horse.
And why do you think he came to your house anyway?

Purple tulips in the adoration chapel

They stand as I ought: one so much like the others
that only the attending florist could tell them apart.
(But I don't want to fit. I want a deeper hand

to lift me out. I want to hear the cry
of God, the flower's encasement groan as it tries
to answer, lying spent on a roadside marge.)

What do we have to offer, but our offending selves?
We are part of the horrible show, in face paint, big shoes.
Sitting in the dirt, we wait for Jesus to pass.

We're a punch line for no joke. What can we do
but repose in what we've become? Our reckoning appears
before it does. (Who else are we going to sit with?)

I want to drink living clean water. Take in
new air. I want to sing the price for my life
in a procession that may never even notice me.

I will be like the tulips: my life in a simple vase,
one voice in twelve, apostles of purple love,
a Jimi Hendricks who leaves the worst behind.

The long rise

It's a long gurney ride; you haven't been forgotten.
Jesus has room for everyone: the ill-mannered, the contrary.
He doesn't feel tested. He can wait for as long as you can.

Who has a mother like this? She delights in you.
She has a heart which is all outdoors. The rain
can come, but the fruit will still be split on the board.

Could you ask for more sun? Could you find greener grass?
You feet, ball and socket, are a dance before
they begin. Your hands might be birds, out a car window.

And Lents, well, they come and go. You are still
a fool. People walk around, ringing His bell.
You'll just have to do your best. (It won't be enough.)

Every dark place has a seat at the end of the hall.
The creak in the walls will answer your ego's call!
(We need to move away from the noise of this world.)

Jesus will tell you when to sit and when to rise.
You'll listen, too. That's your part in this habitation—
to live where you don't, to wake up in a further field.

Take these sins I love

Cravings become charms, amulets, the other answer.
We cry out with half a mouth, an empty cup.
Take this crusting. The sickness is deeper than we know.

The cure is not in my hands. I can't staunch this wound.
God's demands are too much—which, as it turns out,
are exactly what we need! His passion is austere;

His truth in a created circuit lies. He calls for,
repays our praise, will settle for nothing less.
(He's a gentle rain at night, the grass that listens.)

And the Augustinian fire we cry out of? It's the sound
of a Holy Phoenix being born. His pain is ours;
His red wings beat, create an answer, a motif.

(What a rout it'll be. I'll see old friends, my children!
Linda—after she's done with Bach. The whole
of freedom, shining in a tree, a better pear.)

Whole treatises might come out of this, a mother
find her home. It's a weird compass that leads us:
an airy distillation, the sounds we live for.

Lilies of the valley, daffodils

Lent is an early water trickle, it feeds the soil.
The earth is cracked seed, a hand
that reaches up
and violates every countryside.

It's something that owns you;
she knows everybody's name.
She seeps in basements, whispers in our sleep.
She ticks off the time left to us, has an answer,
had one before you came.

Lent is all your dreams and your place in them.

Her schedule is not ours.

Winds blow over the fields near Stockholm

Stockholm is a black stocking,
an orphan's face. She owns miter and crown,
is like a dog who keeps wagging its tail.

Come on in, come on in, you want to tell her.
Come in out of the cold,
but she doesn't live here—doesn't live anywhere.

All our lives we're like her, singing the "o"
in every old ballad, searching for the missing piece.
What we want we cannot find.

To say it finds us is true enough, but we don't live
just in the finding. We live to be found.

The small sound of hammers

You can hear them in the canyon.

No one has a name down there, not yet.
There isn't time for that. The sheriff
wears a star, mostly because he likes how it gleams:
a sun in the sun. That kind of thing.
People are filled with a small resolve; they breakfast
on dried corn flakes, walnut bread.

Someone is putting up a small building—a saloon.
In the center of town a horse snorts along a rail;
generosity ensues, one person, then the next,
and before you know it, civilization.

Jesus could walk down the street,
and no one would notice.

I wouldn't know your name, but that doesn't matter.
A smile is the same in any language. "Rusty . . .
My name is Rusty." Suits well enough—
though it's not quite time for talking.

Pieces are still being put together.

First exercise on the Passion of our Lord

(Agony in the Garden)

1.

Blood sounds, bobs a leaf,
the sky, as the city turns against its sleep.
He tries to keep this to Himself:
the whole earth, dead to the pressures,
this night and the darker realms:
every angel there—He knows their names!

They could rip His shell off His back,
would do so now if not held off.
They would squeeze Him just to hear the give
in His voice: hope, the last straws of it
between their fingers. It is as if they
were at a fraternity party, couples, leaning drunkenly
into the scene, one and then the next—
each for the others; then out again.
The shriek of women pulling babies apart,
their more distant conspiratorial voices.
The slow, deliberate male breaths on his neck
would be too much for anyone,
the maniacally slow whisper of perfumed kings,
having gotten used to their power, sure of it.
They wield the sword. They rule here.
He'd see that before they finished.

2.

His groans would affect me, the dry heaving:
wrench of ribs, obliques—
mostly because I could do nothing.
The burden would be His, worlds conjoined;
all of Him sinking deeper

into what He had to become.

Even if I were to stay awake, how much
could I get out of this? (I would see a suffering
beyond me.) I might move closer, pathetically
try to lift Him straight, my hands under
His armpits, straining, Him collapsing: knees,
groans, as I vainly try to help Him gather Himself.

But that would not be what I am here for.

I'd have to fall back, defeated, feel
for my place, under a nearby tree.

What I have become is lost to no one.

3.

Union is a myth.
St. Catherine, Francis, how could they know God's pain,
though their hands screamed like razors—
though they devoutly embraced the sails
the best find there—bent points
that caught ground beneath their feet?

I could, perhaps, inch in that direction,
but I cannot be someone else.

I am what I start with, what I end up with.
I cannot give enough—or anything, really.

We sit here. We stand.
It doesn't matter.

4.

Jesus complains to the only men
who'd ever heard: knot-headed fishermen.
They do not.

He rouses them, tells them his soul
is being eaten, that dark hands, a severed
humanity converges: the sweaty grasping,
the slide in that defeated flesh.

We are hopeless, each person
sinking in his own tide, with his list of complaints.
Some are dazed, without heads;
they wooze, fall over, each inching his way;
others, barely coherent.

"You are God," they say. "Hold us."

All Jesus can feel is the press of breath,
those faces: each claw, failing, wanting
a piece of His skin. His heart breaks
because the angels left Him first,
all of creation now, funneling after.

Who could endure this: a day's blue sky
collapsing in on itself, yesterday's newspaper;
the moon turning red as a raised stone;
stars dying because they want to,
because of what men will do,
whatever His sacrifice.

He convulses because He only has a body
to answer with; he sweats blood
because the world is thirsty, because sin
is preparing a sop for all of us.
The devil licks his fingers—
His Father's further art.

How many will ignore this night,
go right on burning.

5.

He stood there outside of space, time,
opening a door in the universe.
What happened did not surprise Him.
It could have been wild dogs;
what would have been the difference?

One by one His followers left Him,
one by one, the happy multitude
forgot His works, His opened hands, His mother.

He walked through that.

He woke His three groggy friends, took them
by the hand because they needed to know.
But that would've been a consolation—so

He walked on.

Given up to an agitation that owned Him,
He turned to the last One who would turn away.
He would be what was left: a jellied
plasma, an unformed shaking.

He walked.

On the Shroud of Turin, a negative

the whole world is left-handed:
cheek puffed, His benign strength.

My sins are like a pile of bruised apples,
the rotting smell of uncollected cider.
(This is how I walk around!)

I'm like that Hungarian guy:
George Gabor, who impersonated a fictional
European industrialist,
Baron Frederick von Krupp, in 1926.
Harvey Firestone Sr. went out of his way
to show him both belonged—in Akron.

They did.

But the thing is, the impulse inverts:
Gabor couldn't stop performing,
got arrested, deported every time
he came back to America.

Maybe he enjoyed that part of it, too,
maybe he waved at the press
as they cuffed him, walked him back home.

The heart of God is torn

and so is open. The lance just made sure.
(Every dad knows the cost of doing business.)

God is Lent: the hand that reaches out to Adam
on the Sistine ceiling beats in blood.

*

He's been to work all day, comes home
with an empty lunch bucket. Silent as his step
up the front walk; dehumanized,
he slowly comes alive. The odor of the shop fades.

His childlike joy enlivens the room.

These might be memories; either way,
they are true. The Father comes
and we slam all the doors down the long hallway,
light everywhere. We're hardly on earth.

He delights in this, so many of His kids
crossing each other's paths!

Lent is a green time

—after Crossing the Threshold of Hope

This world oils its glorious machinery—
is its own shout.
It stamps out hard rolls, benefactions.

This Pope, both hands raised to the flock in front of him,
knew this. It's like a giant red sandstone sculpture,
the "Hands of Man," one that could've been left over
from a Communist regime:
one palm deeply involved over the other,
a gesture that reaches both in to and out of God—
praise, answering a tongue
it can only partially hear.

Hope changes us, anchors us in this world.
We use it, like longshoremen or loggers; we make
the new new again, and will for as long as we live here.

This is why we get up each morning.

This is why we remake the bed of earth, pulling its covers
up tight in our call for answers. "Come to us, Lord.
Flex Your muscle, which is ours too."

The pope sits at the foot of mountains.
Someone takes his picture.
Everyone is his friend there, everyone speaks his language.

Hope is a jackhammer

—after JP II

It works through every blessed season,
owns them. It builds with the world in mind.

Your life is a series of duplexes,
not a garret, but a large condominium.
Flowers come and grow.
You must open for new business.

Who will this person be? How can he be?

That's why they throw open the shutters.
That's why every morning has a new face.

You've always carried the road with you,
rolled up in your backpack: a Lent,
this Jesus. Your life will not change much,
just get busier. It will be like the friend
who rips you a piece of his bread,
or gives you a schedule of buses.

All of this in the calm.
All of this marking the time you have left.

Is the house teaching when it
creaks at night?

Only one answer endures.
He's the rain after you go to sleep,
the mist you're not awake to see.
He slowly takes the town's asphalt,
in from the harbor. There's a buoy out there
(which might be your response).

We could go on praising Him, will.
He's the house, the parchment we write on.

The dying part, Him on the cross,
is always here as well.
The green of the grass is infected with it—
as love always involves another.

A doorway takes you down
to an African village, where people jump
when they dance. Someone will offer fruit;
you will learn how to laugh
in another language.

Weariness has no home there.
Your body will be like a large flower,
having its full say in the wind: yellow
against green against yellow.

He might be a friend walking across the street,
or the way you sing when nobody's watching.

All of life is the prayer you want to make.

Palm Sunday

It's a lonely God
who will know more of that
before the week is through.

When God is lonely, do the planets
catch in their flights? Does the future change?
Whose name stays the same?

What can you give to a king, curling in the dust?

You've played your part: palms waving,
your good will, for as long as that endured.

"Hosanna," your voice a little softer now,
your rank, more assured.

It's time to live with who you are.

*

Let's lift them higher.

This is us, yes, but we are all we have to give.
We are the broken, people most would choose
to forget. We live in corners, in boxes.
We spend our lives among our betters.

We are children of Mary, the shepherds.
No one here has ever called us by our name.
We stood by his cradle.
We stand by Him now.

Jesus, we wave a world You've made.
We wave our dead, shoes we can never fill.
Count us among your chosen, those

who wander in the desert.
Count us among the skid row-ers in Los Angeles;

teach us how to walk down the street.

The Apostles came out

of the house, or a field, one by one.
They were like lice, some thought, ill-equipped.

They crawled all over the bread.

They lived in a smaller place. They knew dust,
betrayal. They did not think in large terms.
How could they, ever? When He spoke,
He was like the sun giving life to the grasses,
or the white clouds high above—the glare.
When He walked on water, they were left
empty. Nothing made sense.

Yet where He moved, people lived, always.
It was like a wind, something that brought life
to the trees. Talk enlivened,
there was more laughter.

Why were they there?
Who in God's name could be?
The rabbis were as bereft as they. The stones
in the buildings were no better off;
somehow they, too, had changed—the grains
thickened. Stories followed, tried to explain,
settle things. But that could not be.
He was why they all were there.

Some nights now, after He slept,
they had to face the truth, who they were
without Him. They could not go back, ever.
Their own families had become a small part of this.

Either He would ride in the new age, or He would,
what? How could He leave them?
How could that be possible? He was still a man,

but not. He was the first and only of His kind.

The future, even if it came, did not matter.

And if He didn't die, how could they?
Yet their fingers still ran along the rough stone,
the sill of barred windows. Tiny pebbles
came off on their hands.

Nothing like this had ever happened before.

Let them be swept up.
Did Moses feel this way, they wondered,
though his bush had no legs, no arms
to gather them in?

Quiet Wednesday

It's like He had gathered all of Himself—
just to stop. He played with some kids,
His legs dangling from a ledge.
He fixed a table, ate and laughed as usual.

Made me anxious.

I walked outside the city gates.
No one seemed happy.

It became clear to me that everything gathered
could be lost. So I walked farther,
out to where sand wraps your feet in wind,
out to where there's more space than people.

I have never had much to give.
The world is large. Me, not so much.

I heard the laughter of painted women.
The city's wares, danglers everywhere.

There was nowhere else to turn.
There never had been.

Thursday, early

If He wants me to die, I'll die.
I don't know what's left to us anymore.
I hear a rooster crow.

He will make things new.
It's what He's always done: bread
will turn into wine. Too many stars will fall.

Something is at hand.

I cannot find Him. The brothers have gathered
somewhere new. I missed the message.

This has happened before, my penchant
for loss, I suppose. When I sit and wait,
He's always come, though today might be different.

Who can always be there,

though once you've gathered with Him,
where do you go then?

Notes

Where we live

"Jocund company" is Wordsworth's phrase.

Bears huddle close in the cave

The Wright reference refers to Franz Wright's poem, "Year One."

Invitation to soybeans

Newman is Alfred E., muse for *Mad Magazine* and for a generation.

Getting the band back together

"Foot it"—lifted from Yeats.

Also, "made new" is a turn on the WC Williams, Ezra Pound Modernist directive.

Saint Valentine's Day

"Aspi" is short for Asperger's, a name no longer favored by professionals in the field. Now it ASD, "Autism Spectrum Disorder."

Burnt Sienna unmade me

"Burnt Sienna" is both a color painters use and a reference to a character in Dante's *Purgatorio, 5*.

Dickinson's death poems are distinctly Protestant in that there is no immediate judgment after death. Guess this turns Donne—"After the first death, there is another." May we all be spared that.

Loud joy

Bishop Barron talks about the term "Ekstasis" in one of his *Pivotal Players* videos. There he says it's the nature of God to be ecstatic, to move out; and he makes the further point that it's a sign of health we should all exhibit. Sin, on the other hand, involves more of a fussy turning inward, a caving in on one's self.

Where Jesus lives

In "Song for St. Cecelia's Day" Dryden untunes the sky.

St. Francis, the inmate, slept here

The "inmate" does not correspond in Hopkins' "The Valley of Elway."

Homer's Cimmerians

These folks apparently preferred dark and gloomy places in *The Odyssey*. Fittingly, they lived along the fringes of his map.

Lent ain't been no purple chair

The title is lifted from Langston Hughes' "Life ain't been no crystal chair."

Purple tulips in the adoration chapel

Jimmi Hendricks recorded "Purple Haze," though I remember him best for "All along the Watchtower." (I left Prince out of this because I think the 80s were simply a terrible mistake, especially as far as hair styles went.)

Take this sin I love

"[I]n a created circuit lies" is a lift and turn of a Dickinson phrase.
The pear comes from St. Augustine's *Confessions*.

First exercise on the Passion of our Lord (Agony in the Garden)

This is based on one of St. Ignatius's exercises.

On the Shroud of Turin: a negative

It's been pointed out that the picture of our Lord is a negative, that is, we see things backward. It must be so. Otherwise the men who punched Jesus's face would have all been left-handed. (Only some of them have been.)

The "sinister" and "gauche" have taken enough abuse. Back when I was a kid, the wise men of baseball had somehow come up with the idea that left-handed people were "flakey." I would have preferred a word like "opposed."

Lent is a green time

While writing this poem and the one that followed, I came across St. John Paul II's *Crossing the Threshold of Hope* for a second time. And since I don't really believe in chance, I tried to allow something of his full spirit to get into two poems.

The apostles came out

Speaking of happy chances, a voice of one of the apostles seemed to come out in these last three poems. I was very happy with that as we seldom think of how completely mind-blowing walking around with Jesus had to have been. No one had ever spoke or acted this way; miracles had become the norm. (Where are you supposed to stand when something like that happens?)

Jesus, thankfully, changes all of our lives, but these guys got both barrels.